The Great Escape

Elizabeth A. Yoder
Illustrated by Kathryn Mitter

Rigby®

A Harcourt Achieve Imprint

www.Rigby.com
1-800-531-5015

Literacy by Design Leveled Readers: *The Great Escape*

ISBN-13: 978-1-4189-3916-8
ISBN-10:   1-4189-3916-1

Printed in China
1 2 3 4 5 6 7 8 985 13 12 11 10 09 08 07 06

Contents

Chapter One
The Animal Shelter

Pierre smiled at Whiskers, and Whiskers looked back at Pierre without blinking. Pierre whispered, "This is a great home for you to live in—it's much better than that old, empty house where you were found today. You have plenty of space, people bring your food right to you, and even though you have noisy neighbors, they'll be good company for you."

Whiskers was curled up on a blue and green plaid pillow on the floor. He looked at the wall for a minute, carefully considering what Pierre had told him. Finally he looked back at Pierre and responded with a quiet *meow* as he flicked his long, fluffy tail.

"Well, I'm glad you agree with me," Pierre smiled. "As soon as I've finished cleaning out your litter box and feeding your neighbors, I'll need to talk to the new volunteer when she gets here." Gently, Pierre scratched the big cat behind its ears and quickly finished cleaning out the litter box. "Mr. Conovas will be here to check on you soon." Then Pierre carefully closed the wire door behind him and went down the short, narrow hall to wash his hands.

Pierre was almost finished with another Saturday volunteering at Porter City Animal Shelter. He had applied to be a student volunteer at the shelter when he was twelve, and he had worked there for a year. Mr. Conovas made sure that all of the student volunteers were following directions and doing their jobs, and also that they got help if they needed it.

Pierre liked Mr. Conovas for two reasons, and the first was that Mr. Conovas called Pierre *Mesye Toussaint*, which is Haitian Creole for *Mr. Toussaint*. Even though Mr. Conovas couldn't understand the language, he enjoyed listening to Pierre speak Haitian Creole to the animals. The second reason was that Mr. Conovas trusted Pierre and knew that Pierre was good at his job and would take care of the animals.

Mr. Conovas was at the shelter every day after school while the student volunteers were working. Each student volunteer worked on a different day of the week. The volunteers who had enough experience and proved that they were responsible were asked to come on Saturdays, too, when the small shelter was very busy.

Most of the student volunteers weren't ready to come on a Saturday when the shelter was packed with visitors looking to adopt the perfect cat or dog.

Pierre volunteered on Wednesdays, and he and his friend Arturo, who volunteered on Thursdays, were the only two student volunteers who came on Saturdays.

Pierre saw Arturo wave to him from the back door of the shelter, and Pierre heard his friend say, "I'm about to walk Giant, so wish me luck!" Pierre watched Arturo push open the door, and before it closed all the way, Pierre could hear loud barking coming from outside.

Giant had arrived three weeks ago, and while he seemed difficult to manage (he was very tall and extremely strong), he was one of the friendliest dogs that had ever come to the shelter.

Unfortunately Giant liked to jump excitedly on Arturo every time he tried to take the huge brown and white dog on a walk, so Arturo had to be careful. The first time Arturo met Giant, he had tried to pet the big dog on the head. Right away Giant had knocked Arturo down and then tried to apologize by licking his face with his rough, wet tongue. Ms. Garza, the director of the animal shelter, and Mr. Conovas had to distract the dog by throwing squeaky toys for Giant to chase.

After that Arturo learned that he could avoid being knocked down by speaking to Giant in a quiet, calm voice, telling the dog to sit, and quickly putting Giant's leash on.

Once Arturo was outside with Giant, Pierre put some dry cat food in the rest of the cat rooms and talked to each cat. He put the large bag of food in the metal bin where the food was kept, closed the lid, and went to the small lobby to wait for Mai Chong.

Mai Chong had attended volunteer orientation the week before, where she learned about the rules and toured the shelter. Today was her first day volunteering, and Pierre would show her all of the things she needed to do during her two hours there. Ms. Garza liked Pierre to show new volunteers what to do because she could trust him to explain things carefully and to answer their questions.

Chapter Two
Changes

The following Thursday, Arturo was putting his old, faded red backpack in the shelter's front office closet when he heard someone call out, "Help!" He quickly closed the door and ran down the hall to the room where the small dogs stayed when they weren't outside getting exercise and enjoying sunny weather.

One wall, painted bright yellow, had several leashes and extra collars hanging on hooks. The wall across from it had ten medium-sized dog crates side by side. Two of the crate doors were open, and a black dog and a brown dog were chasing each other around the room.

A woman with medium-length black hair who Arturo had never seen before was trying to catch the dogs, but they kept wriggling out of her hands.

Arturo called, "Come here, Shadow! Be a good dog!" Shadow ran to Arturo, wagged his tail, and let Arturo pick him up and put him back in his crate. He quickly helped Brownie into the crate next to it.

"Those crate doors don't latch very well," the woman said, and she sounded a little angry. "I latched them, but the dogs just pushed the doors right open and started running around."

Mr. Conovas steered his wheelchair into the room, saying hello to Arturo and nodding toward the woman. "Arturo, this is Mrs. Samson, the new director of the shelter."

Arturo thought back to the previous Friday afternoon when the animal shelter had given Ms. Garza a party before she left for her new job. Everyone was sorry to see her go because she was so friendly to the people and to the animals.

Mr. Conovas smiled at Arturo as he continued, "Mrs. Samson, I'd like to introduce you to Arturo, one of our best student volunteers. He's been volunteering for a year, and Ms. Garza has given him many responsibilities. He'll be very helpful to you while you learn how things work around here."

"It's nice to meet you, Arturo," Mrs. Samson said, "but I probably won't need your help learning how things work here. I have my own way of doing things, and I plan to make some changes. Check your mailbox the next time you're here, because I'm going to print out the new shelter rules and procedures, and I expect every volunteer to read them very carefully."

Arturo frowned in confusion because there weren't any mailboxes for the volunteers at the shelter.

"Mrs. Samson is having someone build new mailboxes," Mr. Conovas explained, "so that she can make sure each volunteer reads any important information that she needs to share with them."

"But we have a notebook that we keep at the front desk," said Arturo. "Ms. Garza always wrote notes and directions to us in the notebook, and we wrote back to let her know about anything that happened while we were working."

"That's a nice idea," Mrs. Samson said, "but I want to be sure everyone has the information they need to keep the animals safe, and I can't be sure that all of the volunteers will take the time to read a notebook."

"We also use it to write notes to each other," Arturo continued. "We've tried other ways to communicate, but the notebook has been the most helpful."

"My newsletter and the mailboxes will be more helpful," Mrs. Samson replied. "Under no circumstances should any volunteer be uninformed." Mrs. Samson scratched one of the dogs behind the ears and then walked out of the room.

As Arturo walked to the front desk to see if Pierre had left him a note, he thought about how hard the volunteers had worked to raise money for the shelter at last month's Pick-a-Pet Day. The shelter didn't have very much money, so everyone was careful not to waste supplies or food. Mrs. Samson's mailbox and newsletter plan sounded like it would cost money—she had to buy materials for the mailboxes and paper for the newsletter—as well as use up space, which the shelter didn't have much of, either.

Arturo found the notebook on the front desk and flipped through it to find that Pierre had left him a short note at the top of the Wednesday page.

Wednesday

Arturo,
I'm worried about the new arrival. It might be hard for others to get used to the way the new arrival behaves.

Pierre

Arturo knew that no new dogs or cats had arrived at the shelter in the past week, so Pierre could only be talking about one new arrival: Mrs. Samson. Pierre must have met her the day before, and Arturo could tell from the note that Pierre was worried, too.

Arturo put the notebook down, and he wondered just how different the shelter was going to be with Mrs. Samson running it. Arturo was very good at sensing when he was going to have to work hard to get along with someone, and he was pretty sure that getting along with Mrs. Samson would be a lot of work.

Arturo went to feed the small dogs, and he worried about Pierre. Arturo knew that his friend avoided talking to people he disagreed with, and that Pierre felt uncomfortable talking about things that might make other people angry with him. When Pierre didn't talk, other people didn't really get to know what a great person he was, or how well he took care of the animals.

"I hope Pierre won't avoid talking to Mrs. Samson," Arturo thought.

Chapter Three
A New Routine

When Ms. Garza had been the director of the shelter, volunteers were expected to hang up their things in the closet, sign their names on a list, and read any new notes in the notebook. Then they were free to play with the animals for a few minutes before they began feeding them, cleaning out rooms and crates, and refilling the supply drawers and food bins.

After Mrs. Samson had been at the shelter for a week, the volunteers' sign-in clipboard disappeared, and it was replaced with a box of file folders, one for each volunteer. The notebook from the front desk was replaced by a framed photograph of Mrs. Samson with her three cats and two dogs.

A few days later Arturo opened the drawer Ms. Garza had kept filled with snacks for the volunteers. But instead of finding crunchy granola and sweet raisins, Arturo stared sadly at paper clips and tape.

The day after that, Pierre tried to open the closet to hang up his coat, but the door was locked. He started to ask Mr. Conovas what had happened when he noticed the pile of coats on a chair in the corner of the office. All the changes were making Pierre and Arturo feel like each day was their first day at the animal shelter.

Now that Mrs. Samson kept her coat and other personal belongings in the closet, she made sure it was always locked. When volunteers first arrived at the shelter, they had to find their folders in the box, write what time they got there, what they planned to do while they were there, and sign their names. When volunteers left, they checked off each item on the list so Mrs. Samson would know what they had done that day, and if they didn't finish everything, Mrs. Samson would lecture them about responsibility. They also had to write the time they were leaving to make sure that they stayed as long as they were supposed to, and sign their names again.

Pierre and Arturo weren't sure how Mrs. Samson paid for all the changes she made, but they were pretty sure that she used some of her own money. Pierre told Arturo that as long as the shelter was exactly how she wanted it, Mrs. Samson would probably spend all the money in the world. "Mrs. Samson likes to spend money on changes," Pierre said.

On Wednesday Pierre signed in, and then he looked for Mrs. Samson's newsletter in his mailbox that was in the narrow hallway. He read it while he walked to the meeting room where the other volunteers were waiting.

In the meeting room Mrs. Samson was holding Stripes, her favorite cat, as she explained that the shelter would be open an extra hour on Saturdays. Then she asked if anyone had questions. After the meeting, everyone left the room and went to take care of the animals.

Since Pierre had met her, he spoke to Mrs. Samson only when she asked him a question. Otherwise he just talked to the other volunteers or to the animals. Because he thought that Mrs. Samson was listening to him and would make a new rule about what to say to the animals, Pierre found himself speaking to the animals more often in Haitian Creole.

He used to like going to the shelter twice a week, but Pierre was starting to think that it wasn't as fun as it used to be. He still liked caring for and playing with the cats, but having to learn new rules every day made volunteering seem more like work than fun.

Pierre finished cleaning out one of the kitten rooms, washed his hands, and refilled some of the food bins before he began cleaning the next room. After he finished filling up the container of kitten food, he was walking back to the cat room when he saw an orange ball of fluff run to the front office. He rushed into the cat room and saw four other cats and kittens climbing wire doors, hiding under boxes, and sitting on top of cabinets. Two large cats were hissing at each other, and the fur on their backs and tails was standing straight up.

Just then Mrs. Samson came into the room and asked, "How did this happen, Pierre? Did you forget to latch the doors when you left the room?" Mrs. Samson shook her head and said, "I knew I should have asked Mr. Conovas to stay in here with you instead of showing him the new trick I just taught to Brownie."

Pierre's face felt hot, but he tried not to let his frustration show as he and Mrs. Samson picked up the cats. He thought that if he spoke, he might say something that would make Mrs. Samson even angrier with him.

"I don't feel comfortable with you being in here alone," Mrs. Samson told him after all the cats were safely back in their rooms. "I'm going to ask Mr. Conovas to stay with you when you're here because this can't happen again." She walked out of the room, reaching in to rub a kitten's head on her way out.

"How can she be so nice to animals but so unfriendly to people?" Pierre wondered. "How could she blame me, the one person who is always careful to close the wire doors because I know the latches often get stuck?" She had quickly accused him without having any facts.

A few minutes later, Mr. Conovas came into the room to help Pierre finish the rest of his chores and play with the cats until it was time for Pierre to go home.

Pierre didn't say anything for several minutes, so Mr. Conovas said, "*Mesye Toussaint*, why aren't you talking to Skippy? He always likes it when you brush him and talk to him, and he doesn't seem to purr as loudly when I brush him."

Pierre grinned and said a few words in Haitian Creole to the small, black cat he was holding. Skippy started purring right away, and Pierre felt his cheeks grow cooler and his anger fade. "I asked him who opened his door and how he escaped today."

"He doesn't seem to have an answer for you, does he?" Mr. Conovas asked.

Pierre frowned and said, "No, he doesn't have an answer for me. I know I didn't leave the doors open, though. I wish the cats could talk and tell Mrs. Samson how the doors got left unlatched."

"That would be an interesting story, wouldn't it, *Mesye?*" Mr. Conovas watched as Pierre latched Skippy's door, and he waved goodbye as Pierre walked back to the front desk to sign out.

Chapter Four
Who Did It?

That night Pierre called Arturo to tell him what had happened at the shelter. During math class the next day, Arturo couldn't think about math at all as his mind filled with how different the animal shelter was now that Mrs. Samson had changed all the rules.

Arturo's stomach flipped when he thought about going to the shelter after school that day–he no longer knew what new rules Mrs. Samson would have created today. Now that things had changed, he didn't get to talk to people because he was too busy making sure that he was checking off every task he had completed. He liked his old routine, and he missed talking to the other volunteers and visitors at the shelter.

Natalya, who sat behind him in class, poked Arturo in the back. Their math teacher had asked everyone to pass their homework to the front of the room, and Natalya was waiting for Arturo to take her homework and pass it forward. He quickly grabbed his homework out of his red math folder and handed the whole stack to the student in front of him.

A few minutes later the bell rang, and Arturo went out into the hall and got some books out of his locker before he went home. Then he changed his clothes and left to go to the animal shelter. He thought about what Pierre had told him on the phone the night before, and he wasn't looking forward to seeing Mrs. Samson.

As soon as Arturo got to the shelter, he saw that something else had changed. In the lobby and in the dog room there were more signs that told people to check the latches on the cages three times before leaving the room.

Arturo sat down in the meeting room and waited for Mrs. Samson to begin.

"I have just a few announcements today, but they are very important, of course," she said loudly. "Yesterday, the student volunteer left the latches open in the cat room, and some of the cats got out. Because of this, Mr. Conovas will stay in the room with all student volunteers whenever they are working, just to make sure this doesn't happen again."

Arturo was surprised the others believed that Pierre had left the latches open—Pierre was usually so careful.

Arturo didn't mind that Mr. Conovas was going to stay with him while he did his job. However, he knew it meant that Mr. Conovas wouldn't be able to get as much of his own work done as he usually did. Mr. Conovas was always nearby, but now that he would have to stay with Arturo, he wouldn't be able to help in the front office or show newer volunteers where to find something in another part of the building.

Mrs. Samson finished speaking, and the volunteers went to the different areas of the shelter to begin working. Arturo and Mr. Conovas worked with the dogs together and talked about what had happened the day before.

"I wasn't in the room with Pierre when he closed the doors, but when I talked to him afterward he seemed pretty upset," Mr. Conovas said.

"When I've worked with him on Saturdays, Pierre is always the person who shows people how to latch the doors," Arturo said. "I think that someone else must have left them open."

"That's possible," said Mr. Conovas, "but Mrs. Samson wants to make sure that everyone is more careful from now on. She just wants the animals to be safe."

On Saturday Arturo woke up with a dull ache in his head, so he called the animal shelter and said that he wouldn't be able to come in. He lay on the couch at home and tried to rest, but he couldn't stop thinking about all the problems at the shelter.

At 11:30 that morning the doorbell rang, and Arturo looked out the window and saw that Pierre was standing by the front door.

Arturo opened the door and asked in surprise, "Pierre, what are you doing here?" Why aren't you at the animal shelter? It doesn't close for another two hours."

"I didn't even know you could get fired from a volunteer job!" Pierre cried.

"Mrs. Samson fired you?" Arturo said, his eyes opened wide.

His face was bright red, and his forehead was creased in anger. "I had to ride my bike over here and tell you because you're the only person who would understand," Pierre said.

"Did someone leave the cat rooms open again?" Arturo asked.

"You're the only one who believes that it wasn't me," Pierre said as he walked into the house and sat on the couch. "I was so mad when Mrs. Samson blamed me for it, but I didn't say anything to her because I thought she would trust me even less. Unfortunately, whatever I did or didn't say suddenly didn't matter, because she was going to blame me for anything that happened."

"You would have admitted it if you'd left the doors open," Arturo smiled. "What *did* happen, Pierre?"

"The same thing that happened on Wednesday," Pierre explained. "This morning I cleaned out Happy's room and then went down the hall to wash my hands. I refilled some supplies and when I got back to the cat room, two of the doors were open, and the cats were behind the can where we keep the food. I was putting Skippy back in his room, but Mrs. Samson came in before I caught Stripes."

"What did she say when she saw you?" Arturo asked.

"Mrs. Samson accused me of leaving the doors open again, and then she told me that she couldn't let me volunteer there anymore because it wasn't safe for the animals." Pierre frowned, and said angrily, "She didn't even ask anyone else if they had been in the room. She just assumed it was me and told me to sign out and go home."

"Wasn't Mr. Conovas in the room with you when you closed the doors?" Arturo asked.

"He was in the room, but he was talking to one of the visitors about Whiskers, and he wasn't watching me when I closed the doors."

"Were there other people in the room?" asked Arturo, hoping that someone else could tell Mrs. Samson that Pierre was innocent.

"There were a few people in the room, but everyone was looking at the cats," Pierre answered.

"Well maybe one of the visitors left the doors open by accident. Did you mention that to Mrs. Samson?"

Pierre shook his head and said, "No, I didn't think she'd listen to me, so I just signed out and left."

Pierre talked with Arturo a little while longer and then he went home. Never had Arturo seen Pierre so upset.

Chapter Five
Pierre's Problem

Later that night, Pierre's parents tried to make him feel better by telling him that he could always volunteer at the Oak Village shelter where Ms. Garza worked now. "You're very good at your job," Pierre's mother said. "No matter what happened at the Porter City shelter, Ms. Garza knows you're a good volunteer and would probably be happy to let you work with her."

"You should try talking to Mrs. Samson," Pierre's father told him. Though Pierre knew that it was a good suggestion, he was still too sad about being asked to leave the shelter. He had taken good care of so many different cats that had later gone home with loving families. It seemed that even though he had enjoyed working at the shelter, getting fired made all of the hard work and fun times disappear.

Pierre couldn't sleep very well that night. His cat, Tiger, was curled up near his pillow, but Pierre tossed and turned so much that Tiger went somewhere else to sleep.

Pierre was frustrated with Mrs. Samson for making him leave without having any proof that what had happened was his fault. He was also frustrated because he didn't try to defend himself to Mrs. Samson. Arturo was always better at talking to other people.

Pierre turned over onto his back, thinking that he could always explain things at the shelter or give answers at school. But he couldn't ever think of the right words when he was upset, and he thought that people wouldn't understand him if he tried to say anything.

"Maybe I made a mistake this time," he thought. "I should have tried to tell Mrs. Samson what really happened, because she may have listened to me."

Then Pierre decided that Mrs. Samson wouldn't have listened to him because she wanted everyone to follow her directions and do exactly what she said. Every time Pierre made up his mind one way, a new thought would make him change his mind again. It was very late when he finally fell asleep.

Chapter Six
Arturo Knows
the Answer

Across town that same night, Arturo sat up in bed. He'd been dreaming about being at the animal shelter, and in his dream, Mrs. Samson was in one of the dog crates, and she was yelling, "Help!"

"I know how the cats are getting out!" Arturo cried. He remembered the first time he had met Mrs. Samson in the dog room—she had said that something was wrong with the latches and that the dogs had pushed open the doors and gotten out. But maybe Mrs. Samson only *thought* she was latching the doors the right way. "Could she be the one who let the cats out?" he wondered.

By Monday Arturo's head wasn't aching anymore, so he got dressed and went to school. He tried to focus on what his teachers were saying, and he forced himself to concentrate during his social studies test.

When the bell rang at the end of the day, he knew that he would have to go to the animal shelter and talk to Mrs. Samson. He would go to the shelter early Saturday morning and talk to her before the shelter got busy.

That Saturday morning at 7:30, Arturo got out of his father's car and walked across the gravel parking lot. He was a little nervous, but he knew what he was going to say, and he knew that it was important to say it. He took a deep breath before he opened the door, and he was halfway through the doorway when something made him stop and turn around.

He thought he had seen a cat sitting in the window near the front door. He looked at the window, which was in the lobby, and sure enough, Whiskers was sitting on a small table right below it, watching the birds in a tree outside.

"What is going on?" Arturo asked himself when he heard barking and meowing coming from the back of the shelter.

"Mrs. Samson, where are you?" he called out as he searched the rooms for the director. Cats were climbing on everything, dogs were running around chasing each other, and plants, boxes, supply cans, and papers had been knocked over.

"I'm . . . in the back . . . with the dogs!" he heard her yell. It sounded like she was having trouble speaking, and Arturo worried that she was crying.

Arturo ran to the back of the shelter to the room with the small dog crates. Almost all the doors were open, and only a few dogs were in the room, sniffing around and pulling dog toys out of a box in the corner. He went to the room next door and saw Mrs. Samson lying on the floor with Giant standing over her and licking her face. She wasn't crying— she was laughing!

"What happened in here?" Arturo asked as he pulled Giant away from her and put him back in his crate.

"I'm so glad you're here, Arturo!" Mrs. Samson said, wiping her face off with her sleeve. "When I locked up yesterday evening, everything was fine, but when I got here this morning, all of the animals had gotten out! I came in here first to try to get Giant back into his crate, but I tripped over something and twisted my ankle. I was having a hard time getting up, and Giant probably thought he was helping me."

Arturo helped Mrs. Samson get up, and she leaned on him as he helped her hop over to a chair in the front office.

"I can get the animals back in their cages," Arturo offered, "but I'm going to need some help." The animals had to get back into their cages before anything else happened, and Arturo knew exactly what to do.

He called Pierre and quickly explained what had happened at the shelter. At first Pierre didn't want to come and help because he thought Mrs. Samson might somehow blame him for what had happened. But when Arturo reminded him that Mrs. Samson was hurt and that Pierre knew how to handle the cats better than anyone else, he agreed to help.

Arturo put the dogs back where they belonged, and when Pierre arrived, he easily caught the cats and put them back in their rooms.

Mrs. Samson, who was sitting with her foot resting on a chair and ice on her ankle, said, "Arturo, if you hadn't come here when you did, I would probably still be lying on the floor with Giant licking my face! Thank you for helping me, and thank you, Pierre, for coming and putting all the cats back where they belong." Mrs. Samson adjusted the bag of ice on her ankle, and then looked at Arturo. "Arturo, why did you come in so early this morning? You know the shelter doesn't open until 9:00."

Arturo looked at Pierre and then back at Mrs. Samson. "I wanted to talk to you about what happened with Pierre . . . about the doors of the cages being unlatched." Arturo cleared his throat, and continued, his voice nervously hoarse. "I know that Pierre is always careful with the latches, so I was surprised when he told me that you thought he had left the latches open."

"There wasn't any other explanation for it, Arturo. Pierre was the last person in the room before I went in and—" she stopped talking and looked at Pierre. "Pierre, would you mind helping me into the cat room? Arturo, please come, too."

Pierre and Arturo helped Mrs. Samson limp to the cat room. Mr. Conovas came in through the side door, and when he saw the boys, he gave them a puzzled look and followed them into the cat room.

Mrs. Samson said, "Pierre, please unlatch that door."

Pierre unlatched the door to Stripes's crate and opened it, and Mrs. Samson pulled Stripes out and held him before she closed the door again and turned the latch to the left. The door seemed to be latched shut, but Mrs. Samson pulled lightly on the handle and the door came open easily.

The two boys looked at Mrs. Samson, whose face was bright red. "Pierre," she said as she stroked Stripes's chin, "I'm so sorry I blamed you for the animals getting out. All along *I* was the one who was leaving the doors to the crates unlatched."

Mr. Conovas put a hand on Pierre's shoulder and said, "I knew there was a good explanation. You knew there was a good explanation, too, right, *Mesye Toussaint?*"

Pierre nodded, and he knew that he finally had to tell Mrs. Samson how he felt. "I know you've been trying to make things better around here, but some of the new routines make things harder than they were, not easier."

Mrs. Samson waited for him to finish.

"I used to be really excited to come here, but lately I've been feeling like I don't even know how to do my job anymore. Then you told me I had to leave, and I was really upset. I want to come back to work here, but it's hard when the rules keep changing."

"I guess I was trying so hard to make this place perfect that I didn't realize it worked pretty well already," Mrs. Samson admitted quietly. "I was so busy making sure everything was the way I wanted it that I didn't notice the new routines were making other people upset."

"Perhaps we can combine some of the old routines with some of the new ones," Mr. Conovas suggested with a smile. "Any ideas?"

The boys smiled, and a few minutes later, they were all at the front desk, watching Arturo throw the sign-in folders into a large garbage can.

Mrs. Samson looked at Pierre. "Would you please come back and be our cat care-giver again? You've shown me today that you really are the best one for the job!"

"I will if you'll do one thing for me," Pierre said. "In your next newsletter, add that latches should be turned to the right and not the left!"